The Official
Chelsea FC
Annual
2008

Written by Rick Glanvill

A Grange Publication

© 2007. Published by Grange Communications Ltd., Edinburgh, under licence from Chelsea Football Club. Printed in the EU.

Photographs © PA Photos & Runtings.

ISBN 978-1-905426-81-2

£6.99

D0551110

Contents

Season Report   6

National Dis-Dress!   10

Terrace Anthems   11

Meet the new boys   12

Roll of Honour   14

Blue said that?   16

Carling Cup Glory   18

Word Search   21

Goal Celebrations   22

Breakthrough Blues   24

The Man to Conquer Europe?   26

The Right Stuff – Giving Something Back   30

African Cup of Nations Ghana 2008   32

An Insider's Guide To The New Training
Ground At Cobham   34

Who DID... Eat All The Pies?   36

Cobham 2007 – Beijing 2008?   37

Player Profiles   38

'Don't do this at home' with Billy Blood 45

Record Breakers   46

JT – Chelsea's Captain Fantastic   54

Crossword   56

Spot The Ball   57

Chelsea Goal of the Season 2006/7   58

Quiz Answers   60

Introduction

You have in your hands a very precious item – the Official 2008 Chelsea Football Club Annual.

Inside you'll find even more features, fun, quizzes, poster pictures and fascinating facts about the club we love.

There are profiles of star players and features on ones for the future – youngsters making the big breakthrough as well as all the brilliant new signings made in the summer.

We also sneak inside the new Cobham training complex and look back on the great days last season that made us mighty cup kings.

So while Chelsea aim to be champions in the Premiership and Europe, we hope you'll agree that this is top of the league as far as club annuals go.

Enjoy it!

Season Report →→→→

2006/7 Transfers

Hello to: Michael Ballack (Bayern Munich), Khalid Boulahrouz (Hamburg), Ashley Cole (Arsenal), Henrique Hilário (Porto), Salomon Kalou (Feyenoord), Mikel John Obi (Lyn Oslo), Andriy Shevchenko (AC Milan).

Farewell to: Carlton Cole (to West Ham), Asier Del Horno (Valencia), Damien Duff (Newcastle), William Gallas (Arsenal), Eidur Gudjohnsen (Barça), Robert Huth (Boro), Maniche (loan ended), Lenny Pidgeley (Millwall).

See ya later!: Hernán Crespo (loaned to Inter) and Glen Johnson (loaned to Pompey).

August

Sheva scores on his debut but Liverpool edge the FA Community Shield … injuries to Cech, Gérémi, Makelele, Gallas, Ballack, Joe Cole and counting … Man City makes Cudicini's 79th clean sheet for the Blues, second best record in our history … hamstrung Robben withdraws in the warm-up at Boro, and a shock defeat follows … fantastic win at Blackburn with the new boys looking great. League position at end of month: 4th.

September

Hasselbaink scores at the Bridge for Charlton – and apologises to the adoring crowd! … Ballack's first goal (a pen) and a great start to the Champions League … cracking winner against Liverpool from on-fire Drog … 'beat your neighbours' is easy-peasy at Craven Cottage … Drogba nets his first ever Chelsea hat-trick in Bulgaria … 10 shots on target but frustration against Villa. Position: 1st.

October

Seventies legend Peter Osgood's ashes laid to rest at the Shed End … double keeper injury horror at the Madejski Stadium … memorable victory over Barca … under-fire Sheva and Ballack see off Portsmouth … Kalou's first goal starts the Carling Cup charge at Ewood … Hilario saves a pen and Lampard stars at Bramall Lane … brilliant strikes from Lamps and Drog silence the Barcelona fans in an epic match. Position: 2nd.

November

JT sent off and league defeat at Spurs for the first time since 1989! … storming Carling Cup win over Villa, who bussed fans to the Bridge for free … another four against Watford, with Drogba's second hat-trick of the season … Gérémi's surprise free-kick ends West Ham's resistance … disappointment in Germany but still on course to qualify for the Champions knockout phase … second-half pummelling of United brings only the draw … Ballack header breaks the deadlock at Bolton. Position: 2nd.

December

Into the knockout rounds in Europe with an easy win over Levski – SWP gets his first ever Chelsea goal … Mourinho names his 'untouchables': Essien, Makelele, Lampard, Terry, Carvalho, Ashley Cole, Drogba, Ballack, Cech … right-back Essien's exocet missile salvages a point against battered Arsenal … Drogba almost single-handedly sees off Newcastle (twice) and Everton – including yet another wonder goal … Robben marks his return to fitness with a last-minute heartbreaker at Wigan … JT is out after back op … Drogba gets his 50th goal in blue, but it's two disastrous home draws at Christmas. Position: 2nd.

Season Report

January

Chelsea let leaders Man United off the hook with stalemate at Villa Park ... Lamps grabs a hat-trick and Mikel his first against Macclesfield in the FA Cup ... plucky Wycombe eventually seen off in the Carling Cup semi – Cardiff here we come! ... Diarra lays claim to problem right-back slot ... . Wigan trounced with Mikel starting to shine ... though Cech returns, injuries take their toll at Anfield ... Forest felled in the FA Cup ... Ashley Cole stretchered off in the crushing of Rovers ... transfer window shuts with no new arrivals. Position: 2nd.

February

JT returns in professional beating of Charlton ... sweet, Robben-inspired revenge against Boro puts us 10 points clear of third-placed Liverpool ... SWP takes Norwich apart in the Cup – our 5th 4-0 of the season ... hard-fought draw in Porto sets up tough second leg ... JT is knocked cold, but it's a glorious win in the Carling Cup Final as Drog grabs a brace ... Chelsea become the last team to win a major trophy at the Millennium Stadium ... United go nine points clear. Position: 2nd.

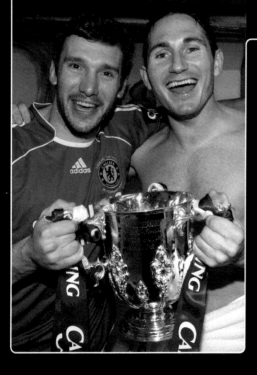

March

Chelsea win 2-0 at Portsmouth for the 4th season running ... Robben makes the difference in the second leg against Porto ... Lampard and Kalou are the heroes as Spurs are pegged back in the FA Cup quarter-final ... now Essien's injured ... struggling City offer little resistance ... Blades blunted by Sheva's early strike and Lamps's 20th goal of the season ... the Ukrainian and SWP top an awesome FA Cup replay performance at White Hart Lane ... showdown with United at the Bridge – scheduled for FA Cup semi-finals weekend – is postponed ... Kalou's late, late header at Vicarage Road just about keeps title hopes alive. Position: 2nd.

April

Valencia earn a tight draw at the Bridge … Joe Cole finally returns from injury … Riccy's screamer settles the tussle with Spurs and leaves us three points short of Man United … again switched to right-back, Essien delivers the killer blow late in Valencia – semis here we come! … Ballack kills off plucky Blackburn in extra time and sends us into the FA Cup Final at new Wembley … SWP double buoys tired Blues at Upton Park … desperately disappointing performance at St James' Park damages our Premiership chances … despite domination, there's only a Joe Cole winner to take to Anfield for the Champions League semi-final 2nd leg … party-poopers Bolton sneak away from the Bridge with a point. Position: 2nd.

May

Champions League semi-final despair again - dumped out at Anfield in a penalty shootout … Blues rally brilliantly at the Emirates after Boula's sending-off but it's not enough – the title is Man United's … lack-lustre league encounter with United ahead of our FA Cup Final meeting … Everton grab surprise draw as Chelsea's minds are elsewhere … Chelsea triumph over United at the new Wembley thanks to Drogba, who else? He's scored all our final goals in a historic clean sweep of domestic cups. Final league position: 2nd.

National Dis-Dress!→→→

When Didier Drogba was crowned 2006 African Footballer of the Year, he collected the award wearing traditional Ivory Coast robes.

If it's good enough for Africa, it made us think about trying the same thing with the Premiership Footballer of the Year award. Maybe the winner should be made to wear something very, very English when they get the trophy.

So how about Frank having to wear a Beefeater uniform, or Cristiano Ronaldo dressed up as a Morris Dancer?

Fun Stuff

Terrace Anthems (The Clean Versions)

It's great fun having a singsong at Stamford Bridge, but the air turns a bit blue with some of the regular chants. So we've decided to provide you with alternative words for some of our most popular Chelsea songs so you can join in without upsetting your parents.

'We look down on Man United
We look down on Man United
We look down on Man United
As the boys in Blue go on on on!'

'Beat 'em all, beat 'em all
United, West Ham, Liverpool
Cos we are the Chelsea
And we are the best
We are the Chelsea
Who beat all the rest
Beat 'em all, beat 'em all
Etc'

'He's here
He's there
We're not allowed to swear
Joey Cole
Joey Cole'

'Carefree
Wherever you may be
We are the famous CFC
And we don't care
Whoever you may be
Cos we are the famous CFC'

Magic Eye-Mirates

Remember those old 'Magic Eye' pictures? If you gazed long enough at them a mystery image would pop up. Arsenal fans have been told if they keep looking at this picture, it might eventually turn into a Premiership title. (Not much chance of that with the Blues about!)

Fun Facts

John Michael Obi called himself 'Mikel' after journalists mis-spelled his middle name that way at the 2003 FIFA Under-17 World Championships. He liked the sound of it!

Wayne Bridge is a fanatic for the sci-fi movie series 'Star Wars'. His partner bought him a storm trooper's uniform and he wears it a lot.

Meet the new boys

Claudio Pizarro

Born: 3 Oct 1978, Callao, Peru.

Transfer fee: Free.

Former club: Bayern Munich.

Position: Striker.

Honours: Peru international; Bundesliga 2002/3, 2004/5, 2005/6, German Cup, 2003, 2005, 2006, Intercontinental Cup, 2001, all with Bayern Munich.

What he brings to Chelsea: Heading ability, link play and goals. "Pizza" likes the ball played to his feet and is at his best partnering another striker. He was ninth highest scorer in 2006/7 Champions League with four goals.

Mad fact: Claudio owns lots of racehorses, including Raymi Coya, whose stallion father was called Van Nistelrooy!

Steve Sidwell

Born: 14 Dec 1982, Wandsworth, England.

Transfer fee: Free.

Former club: Reading.

Position: Midfielder.

Honours: England Under-21; Championship winner, 2006, PFA Championship Team of the Year member, 2004/5, 2005/6, with Reading.

What he brings to Chelsea: Energy, consistency and great distribution. Steve was one of the outstanding performers in Reading's successful 2006/7 Premiership campaign, running the midfield like a general and harassing opponents.

Mad fact: Steve has a 100-word tattoo on his back that is a copy of the wedding vows he made to his wife Krystall in 2005.

Tal Ben-Haim

Born: 31 March 1982, Rishon LeZion, Israel.

Transfer fee: Free.

Former club: Bolton Wanderers.

Position: Defender.

Honours: Israel international; Israeli Premier League champion with Maccabi Haifa, 2002/3.

What he brings to Chelsea: Experience, power, defensive solidity. Although he is technically excellent, Tal is not afraid to put his foot in where it hurts and is very good in the air. He'll be vital for the Champions League squad.

Mad fact: Tal is a close friend of the famous spoon-bender Uri Geller, and often asks him for advice on his career.

Florent Malouda

Born: 13 June 1980, Cayenne, French Guiana, South America.

Transfer fee: around £13m.

Former club: Olympique Lyonnias (Lyons, France).

Position: Winger/forward.

Honours: France international; French Championship winner, 2004, 2005, 2006, 2007, all with Lyons; French Footballer of the Year 2007; World Cup finalist.

What he brings to Chelsea: Pace, trickery, width, scoring opportunities, and goals. Played with Didier Drogba at Guingamp and with Michael Essien at Lyons, and was one of the most wanted men in football last summer: Chelsea beat Real Madrid and Liverpool to his signature. Has watched games at the Bridge as a fan too.

Mad fact: Florent is from a football bonkers family. His dad was a successful striker in French Guiana and his mum helped start the women's football league there!

Thanks and farewell Gérémi and Magnus

José Mourinho lavished praise on brilliant squad player Gérémi after his summer departure to Newcastle. 'He was an important person and somebody we love very much,' he said. 'He is somebody we miss very much.' Gérémi joined us in 2003 from Real Madrid and won every domestic club honour with the Blues. Former Celtic and Coventry goalie Magnus Hedman was brought out of retirement by Chelsea in November 2006 following the twin injuries to Carlo Cudicini and Petr Cech. He never got further than the bench, but he loved being part of the club and became a hugely popular member of the squad. Cheers Gérémi and Magnus!

Roll of Honour ⊱──⊱──⊱

Chelsea's Players of the Year, 2006/7

In the middle of May, just before the FA Cup Final, Chelsea honoured the best performers of the season in the categories of Player of the Year, Samsung Players' Player of the Year, Young Talent of the Year, Outstanding Achievement and Goal of the Season. It was a night of fun and glitter, and it was hosted by Sky Sports' Matthew Lorenzo and BBC presenter Gabby Logan. The whole thing was broadcast live too, on Chelsea TV. It was hard to disagree with the people who won, but maybe there were others over the season who deserved to win something too, such as Ricardo Carvalho, Scott Sinclair or Frank Lampard.

Player of the Year:

Michael Essien

This is the award the players covet, because it shows how popular they are among the toughest critics – the fans. It is voted for in a massive poll extending from season ticket holders who read the matchday programme to worldwide followers on the internet. The softly spoken Ghanaian was outstanding all the way through a difficult season and adapted brilliantly to lots of different positions, from right-midfield to centre-back. He probably got quite a few extra votes when he scored those fantastic goals against Valencia and Arsenal (twice)!

'I am really surprised,' he said when he received his award. 'I am really happy for this though. I have to thank the fans and the credit goes to my team-mates. They have been fantastic this season.

'I have had to fill in a lot of space, right-back, centre-half, and I did everything for the team. We are all happy for the season. I have enjoyed every moment of it. It has been really hard for us and I think we deserve credit.'

'He's such a powerful player that you could play him almost anywhere in defence and midfield and he is going to do a good job. In the midfield, no doubt at all - world class.' 1975 Player of the Year Charlie Cooke on Michael Essien.

Michael's wicked long-range curler against the Gooners at the Bridge also earned him the Goal of the Season trophy. 'I meant to do it,' he insisted. 'I called to Frank [Lampard], he gave me the ball and the first thing that came into my mind was to shoot. They are one of our big rivals so to score a fantastic goal against them is nice. But I am surprised it won.'

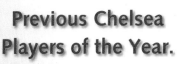

Samsung Players' Player of the Year: Didier Drogba

It would have been a huge disappointment if Didier had come away from the evening with nothing after his fantastic goalscoring exploits. But he's got more to his game than hitting the net. No one gives rival defences a harder time all round, and his defending at corners and free kicks is incredible. What a leader. No wonder his teammates wanted to honour him!

Young Player of the Year: Mikel John Obi

The young Nigerian turned 20 during the season but looked like an old hand once he began to establish himself in the first team. Tall, strong, cool on the ball, his passing became an important part of the way the team played in the second half of the season. Just think how excellent he will be after a few more years in the Premiership!

Outstanding Achievement: Petr Cech

When Petr was seriously injured in the challenge by Reading player Nicky Hunt it was a blow to him and his family but also to the Chelsea team. His determination to get fit as soon as possible was remarkable and he returned in January to put in some fantastic displays in the Chelsea goal once more. He is surely the world's best goalie, but the award was in recognition of his recovery from injury. 'Everyone was looking out for me,' said Petr, 'everyone helped me when I was in a difficult situation and everyone involved in Chelsea Football Club - supporters, medical department, players - take huge credit for my achievement. They gave me the energy and the motivation to come back as soon as I could.'

Young Talent of the Year: Ben Sahar

At 17 Ben Sahar is Chelsea's youngest ever full international. He still has a lot of hard work ahead of him to make it as a top footballer, but he has everything you need to be a top striker: pace, power, movement, height and a knack of finding the back of the net. This could be a very big year for Ben.

Previous Chelsea Players of the Year.

This award has been given every year since 1967. Here are the previous winners.

1967 Peter Bonetti
1968 Charlie Cooke
1969 David Webb
1970 John Hollins
1971 John Hollins
1972 David Webb
1973 Peter Osgood
1974 Gary Locke
1975 Charlie Cooke
1976 Ray Wilkins
1977 Ray Wilkins
1978 Micky Droy
1979 Tommy Langley
1980 Clive Walker
1981 Petar Borota
1982 Mike Fillery
1983 Joey Jones
1984 Pat Nevin
1985 David Speedie
1986 Eddie Niedzwiecki
1987 Pat Nevin
1988 Tony Dorigo
1989 Graham Roberts
1990 Ken Monkou
1991 Andy Townsend
1992 Paul Elliott
1993 Frank Sinclair
1994 Steve Clarke
1995 Erland Johnsen
1996 Ruud Gullit
1997 Mark Hughes
1998 Dennis Wise
1999 Gianfranco Zola
2000 Dennis Wise
2001 John Terry
2002 Carlo Cudicini
2003 Gianfranco Zola
2004 Frank Lampard
2005 Frank Lampard
2006 John Terry
2007 Michael Essien

Blue said that? ➤➤➤

There's been a lot to talk about this season. Can you work out who made the following comments about the Blues? The answers are on page 60/61.

1 "Of course, the money is fantastic but when I was a youngster coming through I played for nothing and my attitude hasn't changed since then. Take the money away and I would still be the first player into training the following morning."

2 "If you're not a big club, you choose one competition and you fight in that competition and forget the others. Big clubs - we cannot do this."

3 "Playing Chelsea is as tough a test as you'll get in Europe these days."

4 "Lionel Messi is a world-class player. He's young, and chasing him around has done my back in."

5 "I feel great. I'm just happy to score the first Cup Final goal in the new stadium. If we didn't win this Cup we would be very, very frustrated."

6 "I bought Luna two Chelsea kits, snuck them into the house and put her in one. Elen laughed but took it off and they haven't been out of the drawer since."

7 "If you ask every player, they want to play for Chelsea, for that team. It's one of the best teams in the world so I'm very happy to be part of that."

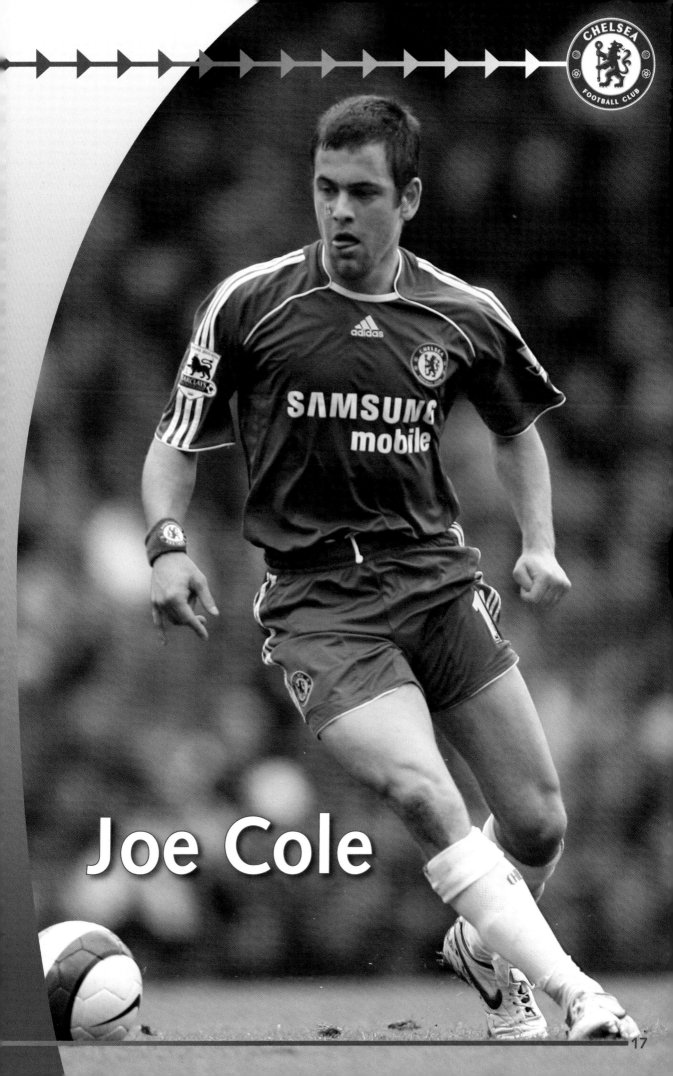

Joe Cole

Carling Cup Glory

We won the last major cup final at the Millennium Stadium, and beat our biggest London rivals too. Remember the events of a great day with these brilliant pictures.

AGAIN!

Chelsea 2   Arsenal 1

Goals: Drogba 2, Walcott
Venue: Millennium Stadium, Cardiff
Date: 25 February 2007
Attendance: 70,073

José Mourinho ✈──✈──✈

Word Search

The surnames of 20 famous Chelsea players are mixed up in the grid below.
They go up, down, backwards or diagonally. Can you spot them all?

```
G K X Y G N I L B M A T N A
W U M H E N O X I D L I W D
I Q L I Y L B G F P V C W U
L W R L D V T V Q E Z D B O
K S H J I D H N N L E O G L
I D I A N T E N E L H O N A
N G L R G P D L E B C G T M
S L T E R R Y L B O E S X Q
I X H L A A E W O O C O Z T
Q K Q P X K H K C L E M O F
Y Z M N A Q E C B V C M L Q
T A N M X I T T E N O B A M
L S E V A E R G N G X T M W
R K K Z P G A L L A C H E R
```

CLUES

Bentley	Gallacher	Makelele	Tambling
Bonetti	Greaves	Malouda	Terry
Cech	Gullit	Middelboe	Vialli
Cooke	Harris	Nevin	Wilkins
Dixon	Lampard	Osgood	Zola

Answers on page 60

21

Goal Celebrations

In 2006/7 Chelsea scored more goals in all competitions than any other season but one in our history. Here's how some of our players celebrate when they find the back of the net.

Frank Lampard. The lunar phases: kiss the ring, point to the moon (Frank's daughter is called Luna, which is Spanish for 'Moon')

Didier Drogba. The Blow Out.

Salomon Kalou. The African Stork.

Michael Ballack. The Do You Know Who I Am?!

Claude Makelele. The 'Where did that come from then, Maka?!'

Ashley Cole. The 'Get in, my son!' (This was for Essien's winner in Valencia – imagine what he'll do when he gets one of his own!)

Michael Essien. The 'S.O.C.O.M.' video game re-enactment.

Shaun Wright-Phillips. The, erm, well, just lose it!

Andriy Schevchenko. The Catch-Me-If-You-Can.

Breakthrough Blues

Lots of young players made their mark at Chelsea in the 2006/7 season. With hard work and a cool head they may make it at the world's greatest club. Read the profiles of our stars hoping for a bright future.

Lassana Diarra

Born: March 10, 1985, Paris, France.
Position: Midfield, right-back.
Chelsea's Young Player of the Year 2006. 'Mini-Maka' overcame disciplinary problems to star in the second half of the 2006/7 season. Pacy, tricky and tenacious.
Breakthrough moment: Porto at home in the Champions League - magnificent in the unfamiliar right-back role.
Possible improvement: Fewer yellow cards.

Mikel John Obi

Born: April 27, 1987, Jos, Nigeria.
Position: Midfield.
Man Utd and Chelsea both fought hard to sign the Nigerian teenager, who made his international debut aged 17. Cool, gifted and strong.
Breakthrough moment: Porto at home in the Champions League - came on for Maka and changed the game with his passing.
Possible improvement: More shots on goal.

Scott Sinclair

Born: March 26, 1989, Bath, England.
Position: Winger, striker.
Impressive in Chelsea's youth and reserve team, went on loan to Plymouth Argyle in January 2007 and blew people away with an 80-yard run and goal against Barnet in the FA Cup. Fast, direct and an eye for goal.
Breakthrough moment: Chelsea Premiership debut against Arsenal in May.
Possible improvement: Chasing back more.

Salomon Kalou

Born: August 5, 1985, Oume, Ivory Coast.
Position: Forward.
Versatile attacker who adapted brilliantly to the Premiership from Holland. Quick-footed, awkward and creative.
Breakthrough moment: Blackburn away in the Carling Cup - made one, scored one, and arrived as a Chelsea player.
Possible improvement: More decisive in front of goal.

Ben Sahar

Born: August 10, 1989, Holon, Israel.
Position: Striker.
One of the highest-rated teenage strikers in the world, and already playing for the national side. Big, powerful and goal-hungry.
Breakthrough moment: Becoming Chelsea's youngest-ever full international for Israel against Ukraine in February 2007.
Possible improvement: Linking with partner.

The Man to Conque
Didier Drogba

Didier Drogba was small and scared when he left his home and parents in Africa for Europe. The idea was for him to quit Ivory Coast and seek a better life with his uncle in Paris. That was 1983. 'I had to travel alone, I was only five,' he said. 'I remember having this thing hanging around my neck, a label saying what my name was, and the stewardess looking after me. It was very, very difficult.'

Having made it as a professional footballer in France, 20 years later he arrived at Stamford Bridge and is fulfilling that African dream. It hasn't all been plain sailing – a section of the crowd booed him at the end of the 2006 season for what they thought was a tendency to tumble too readily in a challenge. But he responded in 2006/7 with his best season yet, ripping defences apart, making other people chances, rallying the team like another John Terry. He's become an inspirational leader.

'I can't say I'm happier because they don't criticise me,' said Didi. 'They have to do it if I'm not playing well. But I just accept the critics. When people know everything about you they can criticise you. When they don't know you very well it's difficult. But that was in the past, now everything is okay.'

In three years he has won every club honour in the English game and become a legend at the club, the first Chelsea player to score 30-plus goals in a season since Kerry Dixon in 1985. But European glory has been tantalisingly out of reach. And after three semi-final disappointments in recent years the Champions League is surely a bigger priority than ever for José, Didi and the rest.

When he signed for Chelsea in 2004 Didi was already known to English football fans for his barnstorming performances as Marseille's lone striker in UEFA Cup clashes with Newcastle and Liverpool. He destroyed the likes of Hyppia and Henchoz single-handedly.

And at Chelsea it was the Champions League stage that gave him the chance to do the same against the very best in Europe, such as Barcelona. 'Those are the games I love,' he said. 'You have to think. You make one mistake and, not always but usually, there

is a consequence. A goal. Both teams are so experienced, the games are very close. I learned a lot about how to play in these games in my first year at Chelsea. That was not my best season, but it was my most intelligent season.'

He was targeted by Barcelona in 2004 and harshly sent off at the Camp Nou. But he has got wiser each season in Europe and nothing illustrates that better than the brilliantly taken last-minute equaliser that stunned the same stadium last season and earned a draw.

'I feel we're not far from winning the Champions League, even if it's not this season then next," the striker said last April. 'The team is getting more experience. We know each other much better and the new players are adapting so even if it is not this season it will be next season. We don't give up and we will win it.'

In his first two seasons, Didi was used as the lone striker between two wingers upfront. He preferred last year, when the arrival of Andriy Shevchenko meant a different formation. 'It's completely different when we play with two strikers,' he said. 'You just have to see the statistics. I score more goals when there are two strikers than I do when I'm alone. That's the difference.'

He is already the most feared striker in Europe. And now that he has his old friend, winger Florent Malouda, alongside him, perhaps he can score even more freely – including, perhaps, the winner in that Champions League final at last.

If he doesn't, it won't be for want of trying.

John Terry

The Right Stuff ✈

Giving Something Back

People talk a lot about Chelsea's success and the money involved in making a football team one of Europe's best, but there's more to being a great club than that.

Chelsea FC believes that sports organisations can be a force for good in troubled countries. In 2006 the club announced that it had chosen a charity partner to help do good things around the globe. That partner is 'Right To Play'.

With events in Britain and abroad, 'Right to Play' and Chelsea FC aim to use sport and play to improve the lives of children affected by poverty, war and disease.

They have established projects designed to teach important skills including leadership, teamwork, respect and fair play. They have fun too. A typical example was the trip to Ghana in June 2007.

Chelsea flew out José Mourinho, coaches including youth Academy manager Neil Bath and Eddie Newton, and young players such as Sam Hutchinson. Also there were Ghana-born youth team player Nana Ofori-Twumasi, former Blue Marcel Desailly, and the star of the show everywhere they went, Ghana international Michael Essien.

Local youngsters in Accra and Tamale were invited to well-organised football training and skill sessions. When news got round, people travelled from miles around to see the Chelsea representatives and watch the sessions. But mostly they aimed to catch sight of national hero Michael Essien – he has made Chelsea everyone's favourite side in the West African country.

José Mourinho loved working with the local youngsters. 'What I have found with these boys is that they are people with big desire to succeed. They know the meaning of the group, the meaning of the friendship, co-operation, solidarity and they are very, very nice people.

'I think we have in Chelsea a great example of what the world is all about. Many different cultures, races and colours but we feel a family, we live as a family and we are a family.'

Teenage Blues defender Sam Hutchinson was left with even deeper impressions: 'It has been one of the greatest experiences of my life,' he said. 'I'll never forget it. All the people are so welcoming.

Playful José explained how a mistake in his training always ends with a flick of the ear. Painful!

José met the Right-Honourable O B Amoah, Ghana's Deputy Minister of Sport – he's a Chelsea fan!

'There is a high standard in football. We speak about Cobham and the lovely pitches, but they are playing on gravel, big lumpy bits of mud, stones on the pitch, and they have got a very good touch, they can see a pass, they are very strong naturally. They are very good players.

'And when you see the reaction to Michael it definitely makes you even more ambitious to make it. He is like a king out here and when you see people getting that admiration, you would just like a little bit of it.

'It was my first time to Africa, it won't be my last.'

The aim of 'Right To Play' is to have a lasting impact on the communities visited. Chelsea left all their training kit and many souvenirs behind for the benefit of tomorrow's Essiens and Desaillys. No one in Ghana will forget the week Chelsea came to town in a hurry.

And who knows, maybe even the Blues tradition of flicking the ear of someone who mucks up in training will catch on too!

Find out more about Chelsea and 'Right To Play' here at *www.righttoplay.org.uk*.

African Cup of Nations

The prestigious African Cup of Nations takes place every two years and lots of Premier League stars play in it. This season it will be staged in Ghana, West Africa, from January 20 to February 10 2008.

That probably makes Chelsea's Michael Essien, Mikel John Obi, Didier Drogba and Salomon Kalou unavailable to the Blues for nearly a month. Still, it also means you can pick a 'Chelsea' team to support in the finals.

Black Star Essien, Super Eagle Mikel

Ghana

Back of the net:
www.ghanacan2008.com

Team: Ghana.
Nickname: Black Stars.
Chelsea connection: Michael Essien.
Why you should support them:
They have the maddest fans.
Prediction: Hosts with the
most – champions!

Ivory Coast

Team: Ivory Coast.
Nickname: The Elephants.
Chelsea connection: Didier Drogba and
Salomon Kalou.
Why you should support them: They
have the wickedest goal celebrations.
Prediction: Unforgettable charge to the
final for the Elephants.

Nigeria

Team: Nigeria.
Nickname: Super Eagles.
Chelsea connection: Mikel John Obi.
Why you should support them: They
have the loudest travelling supporters.
Prediction: Super Eagles brought down
to earth in the quarter-finals.

An Insider's Guide →→ To The New Training Ground At Cobham

It was only right that Roman Abramovich was one of the people who opened the brand new 140 acre training ground and physiotherapy centre at Cobham back in July. After all, he'd paid for it!

The main building has all the latest technology and features. These include an indoor pitch for bad weather, a moat to reflect light into the building, an underwater treadmill with video cameras for injured players to exercise without hurting their joints, eight rest rooms for a quick lie down between press-ups, and a roof covered with grass so it blends into the local landscape!

The new facilities mean we now have the world's best training ground as well as the world's best team. The six pitches are exactly the same as the one at Stamford Bridge, and lucky local youngsters – as well as Chelsea's squads from schoolboys to first team – will get to use some of them.

Roman Abramovich and others watch as Ashley Cole puts the 'HydroWorx' treadmill through its paces at the Cobham training ground. Manchester Utd have a similar machine but it's much smaller.

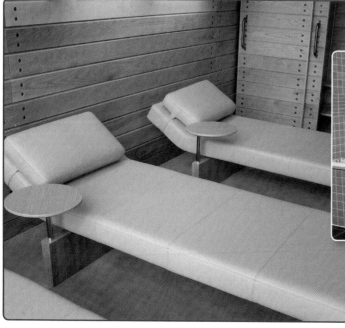

They may look like hotel rooms but the eight rest rooms are there for players to use between exercise sessions. The showers next to the changing room are really powerful and all the shower gel and shampoo you could ever want is provided for free. Pic credit: King Leisure

Temper stands in front of his excellent 'graffiti art' in the players' lounge at Cobham. 'It has been a pleasure and an honour to be a contributor to the facility,' he said. 'I hope the players enjoy the paintings as much as I've enjoyed painting them.' Pic credit: King Leisure

Another great feature in the players' lounge area is a set of six paintings by a brilliant graffiti artist called Temper. He uses spray paints to give his pictures lots of movement and colour.

Real name Arron Bird, Temper first picked up a spray can when he was 11. Now his art sells for huge amounts of money. He enjoyed doing the paintings for Cobham and rates them as some of his most enjoyable pieces of work. 'Everyone at the club has been fantastic with me,' he said at the opening ceremony. 'Of course, I'm a big Chelsea fan now.'

chelsea football club

Who DID...

Eat All The Pies?

The man pictured here is the legendary Willie Foulke, known as 'Fatty' or 'Baby' in his day. He was Chelsea's first ever goalkeeper in 1905/6 and was 6'2" tall, weighing 22 stones – 10 stones more than Petr Cech!

It sounds crazy now, but in 1905 Foulke was the David Beckham of his day. Chelsea was a new club, and they used Foulke's fame in their publicity to capture the imagination of football fans around the country.

At away matches, they would pay men to carry around advertising boards saying, 'Come and watch the 22-stone goalie!' Every newspaper match report mentioned Foulke and how nifty he was around the goalmouth – despite his waist size. 'As agile as a cat,' wrote a reporter after Foulke had saved a penalty in Chelsea's first ever league match at Stockport. That was his speciality. Another opponent who missed a spot-kick was screamed at by his manager afterwards. The player protested: 'But he takes up so much of the goal there was nowhere to kick the ball'.

Chelsea fed stories to the press that built up Foulke's larger-than-life reputation. The papers said once that before an away game, Foulke rose early in the team hotel and found 11 breakfasts laid out ready for when the players got up. Instead, he ate all 11 himself!

Foulke was always a joker. He liked to have his photo taken next to his smallest team-mates to make him look even bigger. In fact, Chelsea 'invented' ball-boys by positioning two tiny lads next to his goal – he used to carry them off the pitch at half-time, one under each arm!

With such an incredible reputation, Foulke was one of the big draws as record crowds turned out to see Chelsea play in that first season.

Sadly, the legend of Willie Foulke lasted just one year at Chelsea. When he returned to the Bridge with his new team Bradford, his former friends put five past him. Cheers!

Foulke eventually retired to run a corner shop in Sheffield. He was never forgotten at Stamford Bridge and a model of him stands in the Chelsea Museum.

How do you think he would have performed in the modern game?

Cobham 2007...
Beijing 2008?

In August 2008, the Olympic Games will be held in Beijing, China. The Games come around every four years. The one after that will of course be held in London in 2012. Who knows, you might get to compete in it if you practice hard enough. We thought it would be fun to imagine some of the Chelsea players taking part in the Olympics – not in football, of course. Can you think of any other sports that one of the boys in blue would be good at?

Michael Essien - Boxing

Look at the size of those fists! Knowing our versatile midfielder-defender, lean, mean Michael could probably knock out two opponents at once. Boxers like nicknames, too, and the 'Bison' or 'Train' is never short of those. Michael's homeland, Ghana, has produced three Olympic medal winners at boxing: two bronze, one silver. We think he could go one step further though. Medal chance: gold

Didier Drogba - High jump

We always knew he had a great leap going for headers... Sorry, though, Didi, only one athlete from Ivory Coast has ever won a medal – Gabriel Tiacoh in the 400m in 1984. Medal chance: bronze.

Petr Cech – Weightlifting

We bet 1970s legend Peter Bonetti never had to lift a load like that! The Czech Republic (and former Czechoslovakia), where Petr Cech hails from, has won three Olympic golds at weightlifting. But you've got to be bulky to lift the top weights, so Petr might struggle. Medal chance: bronze.

Find out more about Beijing2008 at: en.beijing2008.cn.

Player Profiles

1 - PETER CECH

Position: Goalkeeper
Date of Birth: 20 May 1982
Birthplace: Plzen, Czech Republic
Height: 6' 5"
Signed: Jul 2004 (from Rennes)
Appearances: 126
Clean Sheets: 69

23 - CARLO CUDICINI

Position: Goalkeeper
Date of Birth: 6 Sept 1973
Birthplace: Milan, Italy
Height: 6' 1"
Signed: July 1999 (Castel di Sangro)
Appearances: 188 (+5 as sub)
Clean Sheets: 88

> **We have competition almost in every position and I think that is very, very important.**
>
> *José Mourinho on his new squad.*

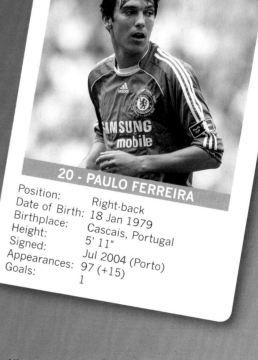

20 - PAULO FERREIRA

Position: Right-back
Date of Birth: 18 Jan 1979
Birthplace: Cascais, Portugal
Height: 5' 11"
Signed: Jul 2004 (Porto)
Appearances: 97 (+15)
Goals: 1

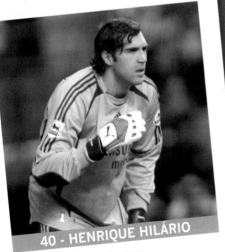

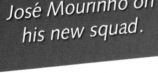

40 - HENRIQUE HILÁRIO

Position: Goalkeeper
Date of Birth: 21 Oct 1975
Birthplace: Sao Pedro de Cova, Portugal
Height: 6' 2"
Signed: Jul 2006 (Nacional Madeira)
Appearances: 18
Clean Sheets: 8

All appearance/goal statistics compiled by Paul Dutton. Correct at close of 2006/7 season.

2 - GLEN JOHNSON

Position: Right-back
Date of Birth: 23 Aug 1984
Birthplace: Greenwich, England
Height: 5' 11"
Signed: Jul 2003 (West Ham)
Appearances: 59 (+10)
Goals: 4

22 - TAL BEN-HAIM

Position: Defender
Date of Birth: 31 Mar 1982
Birthplace: Rishon LeZion, Israel
Height: 6' 1"
Signed: Jul 2007 (Bolton)
Appearances: .
Goals: .

6 - RICARDO CARVALHO

Position: Central-defender
Date of Birth: 18 May 1978
Birthplace: Amarante, Portugal
Height: 6' 0"
Signed: Jul 2004 (Porto)
Appearances: 120 (+5)
Goals: 8

> **Chelsea is one of the top teams in the world so I'm happy to be here. I had to come here and play for Chelsea with the players and staff we have in the squad.**
>
> *Tal Ben-Haim on joining the Blues.*

26 - JOHN TERRY

Position: Central-defender
Date of Birth: 7 Dec 1980
Birthplace: London, England
Height: 6' 1"
Signed: Chelsea youth
Appearances: 298 (+19)
Goals: 31

18 - WAYNE BRIDGE

Position: Left-back
Date of Birth: 5 Aug 1980
Birthplace: Southampton, England
Height: 5' 10"
Signed: Jul 2003 (Southampton)
Appearances: 97 (+11)
Goals: 4

Player Profiles

4 - CLAUDE MAKELELE

Position: Midfielder
Date of Birth: 18 Feb 1973
Birthplace: Kinshasa, DR Congo
Height: 5' 7"
Signed: Aug 2003 (Real Madrid)
Appearances: 172 (+11)
Goals: 2

12 - MIKEL JOHN OBI

Position: Midfielder
Date of Birth: Apr 22, 1987
Birthplace: Jos, Nigeria
Height: 6' 0"
Signed: Jun 2006 (Lyn Oslo)
Appearances: 24 (18)
Goals: 2

3 - ASHLEY COLE

Position: Left-back
Date of Birth: 20 Dec 1980
Birthplace: Whitechapel, England
Height: 5' 8"
Signed: Sep 2006 (Arsenal)
Appearances: 37 (+3)
Goals: 0

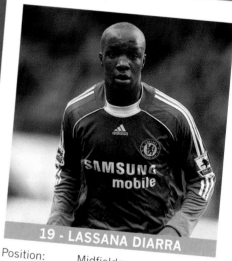

19 - LASSANA DIARRA

Position: Midfielder
Date of Birth: 10 Mar 1985
Birthplace: Paris, France
Height: 5' 8"
Signed: Jul 2005 (Le Havre)
Appearances: 21 (+9)
Goals: 0

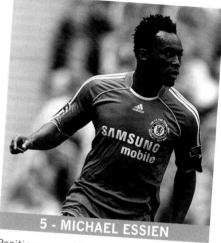

5 - MICHAEL ESSIEN

Position: Midfielder
Date of Birth: 3 Dec 1982
Birthplace: Accra, Ghana
Height: 6' 0"
Signed: Aug 2005 (Lyon)
Appearances: 91 (+6)
Goals: 8

10 - JOE COLE

Position: Midfielder
Date of Birth: 8 Nov 1981
Birthplace: Islington, England
Height: 5' 9"
Signed: Aug 2003 (West Ham)
Appearances: 102 (+66)
Goals: 24

> **"This year we've strengthened the team significantly. The new additions are fantastic."**
>
> *Peter Kenyon at the pre-season US training camp.*

8 - FRANK LAMPARD

Position: Midfielder
Date of Birth: 20 Jun 1978
Birthplace: Romford, England
Height: 6' 0"
Signed: Jun 2001 (West Ham)
Appearances: 310 (+19)
Goals: 90

13 - MICHAEL BALLACK

Position: Midfielder
Date of Birth: 26 Sep 1976
Birthplace: Chemnitz, Germany
Height: 6' 3"
Signed: May 2006 (Bayern Munich)
Appearances: 42 (+4)
Goals: 8

All appearance/goal statistics compiled by Paul Dutton. Correct at close of 2006/7 season.

 CHELSEA FOOTBALL CLUB

Player Profiles

2007/8

9 - STEVE SIDWELL

Position: Midfielder
Date of Birth: 14 Dec 1982
Birthplace: Wandsworth, England
Height: 5' 10"
Signed: Jul 2007 (Reading)
Appearances: -
Goals:

> "When things aren't going right on the pitch or even off the pitch I'm one to really rally the troops and to get their spirits back up."
>
> *New signing Steve Sidwell.*

24 - SHAUN WRIGHT-PHILLIPS

Position: Winger
Date of Birth: 25 Oct 1981
Birthplace: Greenwich, England
Height: 5' 6"
Signed: Jul 2005 (Man City)
Appearances: 34 (+49)
Goals: 6

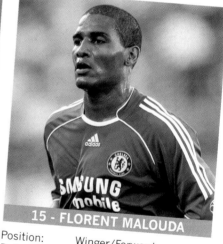

15 - FLORENT MALOUDA

Position: Winger/Forward
Date of Birth: 13 Jun 1980
Birthplace: Cayenne, French Guiana
Height: 5' 11"
Signed: Jul 2007 (Lyon)
Appearances: -
Goals: -

17 - SCOTT SINCLAIR

Position: Winger
Date of Birth: 26 Mar 1989
Birthplace: Bath, England
Height: 5' 10"
Signed: Chelsea academy
Appearances: 1 (+2)
Goals: 0

> "Playing beside such a player is a delight. I know we could find each other on the pitch with our eyes closed."
>
> *Didier Drogba on old friend Florent Malouda.*

11 - DIDIER DROGBA

Position: Centre-forward
Date of Birth: 11 Mar 1978
Birthplace: Abidjan, Ivory Coast
Height: 6' 2"
Signed: Jul 2004 (Marseille)
Appearances: 113 (+29)
Goals: 65

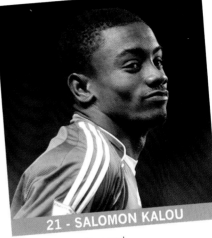

21 - SALOMON KALOU

Position: Forward
Date of Birth: 5 Aug 1985
Birthplace: Oumé, Ivory Coast
Height: 6' 0"
Signed: May 2006 (Feyenoord)
Appearances: 25 (33)
Goals: 9

> **" I have the opportunity to win the Champions League with a great team and a great coach. My goal is to win the Premier League title and all the other cups we'll play in. "**
>
> *New boy Claudio Pizarro.*

14 - CLAUDIO PIZARRO

Position: Forward
Date of Birth: 3 Oct 1978
Birthplace: Callao, Peru
Height: 6 1
Signed: Jul 2007 (Bayern Munich)
Appearances:
Goals:

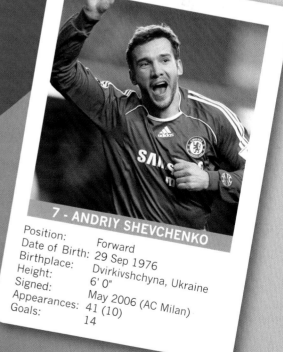

7 - ANDRIY SHEVCHENKO

Position: Forward
Date of Birth: 29 Sep 1976
Birthplace: Dvirkivshchyna, Ukraine
Height: 6' 0"
Signed: May 2006 (AC Milan)
Appearances: 41 (10)
Goals: 14

All appearance/goal statistics compiled by Paul Dutton. Correct at close of 2006/7 season.

PUT YOURSELF IN THEIR BOOTS!

With a behind the scenes tour of Stamford Bridge, home of Chelsea Football Club

BOOK YOUR TICKETS ON-LINE
AT **WWW.CHELSEAFC.COM/TOURS**
OR CALL **0871 984 1955**

'Don't do this at home'
with Billy Blood

To his parents, he is known as Billy McCulloch. But to everyone at Chelsea Football Club he is 'Bill Blood', the club masseur who doubles as squad jester.

If they need geeing up before a big match, or cheering up after one, it's Bill they turn to. He can't sing, he can barely tell jokes, but he'll always give it a go and that's why the players all love him.

Last season, he added another broken string to his bow on Chelsea TV, taking on some mad challenges in front of the cameras, including eating crackers while lying in a bath of fish and baked beans!

We caught up with Billy between jokes, and here's what he had to say:

What's your job title then Bill, dressing room jester or club masseur?

Oi! I'm a sports injury practitioner. Or the masseur.

How did you get to work at Chelsea?

Around 2000, Terry Byrne [now David Beckham's manager] was leaving Chelsea for Watford. He knew me through Steve Slattery, the masseur with the England set-up and Swindon Town, where I was doing sports massage. So Terry put my name forward and I got the job.

What were your credentials as a Chelsea fan?

I'd always liked Chelsea, but working so close with all the players for so long I'm now a massive fan. When I'm working for England the Chelsea lads always start the banter: 'You spend all your time massaging Steven Gerrard!' as if I'm a closet Liverpool fan. But it's not true!

Who are the best Chelsea players to massage?

The England boys really – Lamps, JT (I've got to put him in or he'll get upset), Bridgey, Ash, Coley, Wrighty. Petr Cech's so tall I ought to charge by the yard!

And the worst?

Oh, I'd say Michael Essien. It's like massaging a wall. He's so solid.

Outside Chelsea who would you most like to massage?

I like Nicole Kidman. She'd be alright.

Your best dressing room moment?

Has to be when we won the League the first time at Bolton in 2005. Just incredible scenes. No one could really celebrate though, because we had the Champions League semi-final a few days later against Liverpool. Then unfortunately we lost in that. And the first FA Cup Final at Wembley too. Brilliant.

How did you become the dressing room joker?

When I first joined, like everyone I had to stand up and sing a song. I can't carry a tune very well and chose an Elvis song, 'Only Fools Rush In', and the players started throwing food at me. So I stood there and told jokes instead. No one laughed at first. I thought, 'This is a hard audience'. Then they started laughing. I don't know whether they were laughing at me or with me, but it took off from there really. Now it's a regular thing. I hope it eases the tension. Didier or someone will say 'Come on Bill, tell some jokes' when they think people need picking up a bit. I have to know when to be quiet too.

And now you have your own slot on Chelsea TV …

Yes, and I take challenges from people, so if anyone has any suggestions … I've eaten four chocolate wafer biscuits in a minute while being sprayed with sauce, I've dressed as a diver and taken an ice bath and I've had a bath in baked beans with fish. That was the worst one. I pricked my hand on one of the fins and got ill from it so I couldn't work the following matchday. I'm thinking of doing some for charity in the future.

Finally, tell us one of your jokes.

Bloke goes into a butcher's shop and says, 'Have you got a pig's head?' The butcher says, 'Yes.' So the bloke says, 'Couple of lamb chops then, please … pig face!'

You can see more of Billy at the official Chelsea YouTube page here: *www.youtube.com/chelseafc*

Record Breakers ✈✈

It was a season of ups and downs, but Chelsea wrote new entries in the history books in 2006/7, and the manager and some players created their own personal landmarks. Here, we celebrate their brilliant achievements.

Excluding cup replays that could have happened, Chelsea played **64 games** of the 65 possible at the start of the season. The one that got away was the European Cup Final. Liverpool knocked us out in the semi-final, so we owe them one.

The six **most unavailable players** missed a damaging total of **134** games between them: Joe Cole 38, Petr Cech 27, Arjen Robben 25, John Terry 18, Carlo Cudicini 14, Andriy Shevchenko 12.

Six Chelsea players made **50 or more appearances** in a Chelsea shirt this season. They were Frank Lampard 58+4, Didier Drogba 54+6, Michael Essien 54+1, Ricardo Carvalho 51, Andriy Shevchenko 41+10, Salomon Kalou 25+33.

Only two other clubs have done the **domestic cup double** and won the FA and League Cup in the same season. The others were Arsenal in 1993 and Liverpool in 2001.

José Mourinho proved himself Chelsea's all-time 'Special One' by becoming the manager with the **biggest haul of silverware** ever.

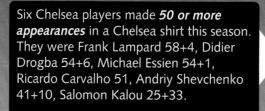

José Mourinho	**(six)** Premiership 2005 and 2006, FA Cup 2007, League Cup 2005 and 2007, Community Shield 2005.
Gianluca Vialli	(five) European Cup Winners' Cup 1998, UEFA Super Cup 1998, League Cup 1998, FA Cup 2000, Charity Shield 2000.
Ted Drake	(two) League Championship 1955, Charity Shield 1955.
Dave Sexton	(two) FA Cup 1970, European Cup Winners' Cup 1971.

José has also **won loads more** in the last three years since he arrived in England than any rival manager in the 'big four'. Tell that to your mates!

José Mourinho – six	(see above).
Rafael Benítez (Liverpool) – four	Champions League 2005 (on penalties), UEFA Super Cup 2005, FA Cup 2006 (on penalties), Community Shield 2006.
Alex Ferguson (Manchester Utd) – two	Premiership 2007, League Cup 2006.
Arsène Wenger (Arsenal) – two	FA Cup 2005 (on penalties), Community Shield 2004.

Chelsea have now **won the FA Cup four times**, putting us 11th in table of all-time winners.

We also won the **League Cup for the fourth time**, making us 3rd in the all-time table of winners.

We were **runners-up in the Premiership** for only the second time. We were never runners-up in the old Football League.

We reached the **Champions League semi-finals** in 2007 for the third time.

Sixty-four games in one season is a club **record number of games played**, beating the previous 61 in 1999/2000. Of the 64, we won 42, drew 16, lost 6, We scored 117 and conceded 43. We managed 33 clean sheets and failed to score on just six occasions.

Forty-two wins in a season is our equal greatest, together with 2004/05.

We achieved our **longest ever unbeaten sequence** home and away of 23 games, beating the 19 completed in 1984, 1998 and 2005.

We were in our **longest ever unbeaten home league sequence** at the end of 2006/07: It was 63 not out so far, equalling Liverpool's all-time top-flight record set between February 1978 and January 1981. Avoiding defeat at home to Birmingham puts us out on our own with the best ever unbeaten home league record. Our last league defeat at Stamford Bridge was the 1-2 defeat to Arsenal in February 2004. In the time since then we have played 63, won 48, drawn 15, lost 0, scored 131 and conceded 29.

The 11 away league clean sheets equalled our club record set in 2004/05 (also a record for the Premiership).

Six defeats in all competitions is the equal fewest in our history, the same as in 1998/99 and 2004/05.

The **six successive away wins** of 2006/7 equalled our top flight record set in 2004/05 (twice) and equalled in 2005/06.

Lampard became the **first to play 50 matches** in Europe for Chelsea.

Frank Lampard made a **record number of appearances** in a season for Chelsea with 62, beating the 59 played by Dutch goalie Ed de Goey in 1999/2000.

Frank Lampard became Chelsea's **top scoring midfielder** of all time with 90 goals. He is currently our 10th highest goalscorer.

Frank Lampard became only the **second player to win 50 caps** or more as a Chelsea player. The other was Marcel Desailly of France.

Record Breakers ✈

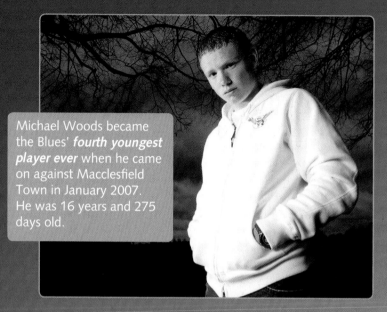

Michael Woods became the Blues' *fourth youngest player ever* when he came on against Macclesfield Town in January 2007. He was 16 years and 275 days old.

Didier Drogba was also the *top scorer in all competitions* with 33, the highest total for a goalscorer at Chelsea since Kerry Dixon's 36 in 1984/85.

He also became the *first African footballer* ever to score in an FA Cup Final game.

Didier Drogba was *African Footballer of the Year*, PFA Player of the Year runner-up, and Football Writers' Footballer of the Year runner-up. Michael Essien came third in the African Footballer of the Year award.

Ivory Coast's Drogba has now scored *more international goals* than any previous Chelsea player.

Wayne Bridge, Ricardo Carvalho, Petr Cech, Didier Drogba, Paulo Ferreira, Gérémi and Arjen Robben all made their *100th Chelsea appearance*.

Didi won the Premiership *'Golden Boot'* for most goals with 20. He's the first Chelsea player to win it since Jimmy Floyd Hasselbaink with 23 goals in 2001.

At 17 years 181 days, Ben Sahar became *Chelsea's youngest ever international* when he played for Israel against Ukraine in February 2007. He became Chelsea's youngest international goalscorer six weeks later when he netted twice against Estonia.

Joe versus Liverpool. This was Joe Cole celebrating his winner v. Liverpool.

José Mourinho **won his 100th Chelsea match** after 142 games.

Didier Drogba reached the **50-goal mark** for the Blues against Reading on Boxing Day 2006.

Chelsea fielded **three goalkeepers in one match** for the first time on record against Reading. Petr Cech and Carlo Cudicini were taken to hospital and John Terry went in goal – wearing Hilário's shirt! (He kept a clean sheet.)

In 2006 John Terry became **Chelsea's first England captain** since Vivian Woodward in 1911.

John Terry and Frank Lampard both passed the **300 appearances** milestone.

With thanks to Chelsea statistician Paul Dutton.

TRUE PASSION.

Become a **Junior Chelsea Member** for the 2007/08 season and get a load of great benefits!

- Priority Access to Chelsea home match tickets ahead of the general public

- Match Tickets at a cheaper rate than those sold on General Sale

- A fantastic Chelsea Junior True Blue Membership Pack containing goodies such as an exclusive Chelsea DVD, Stationary Set, Pennant, Fixture Wallchart and loads more!

So why not join today....
its easy...just visit
www.chelseafc.com or call
0871 984 1905 for an
application form.

Junior Membership costs **£17.50** in the UK.

IT'S IN THE BLOOD.

Michael Essien

Petr Cech

Frank Lampard

JT – Chelsea's Captain

Did anyone have a more eventful last season than John Terry? Made captain of England in September, became emergency goalie at Reading in October, was sent off for the first time in his career at Spurs and then injured in November, got knocked unconscious in winning the Carling Cup Final, scored the first goal for England at the new Wembley, then lifted the FA Cup at the same stadium in May and, finally, married girlfriend Toni Poole in June. Phew!

On the phone call from Steve McClaren that made him captain of England: 'It was a Thursday afternoon and it was being announced publicly on the Friday. When I got the phone call I was having a massage at the club when my phone rang, private number. For some reason I never answer private numbers, I just cancel them. And I let it ring and it kept ringing and ringing. I answered, "hello", and it was Steve on the other end. He said, "John, I've got some good news, I'm going to make you my England captain" and for once in my life I was gobsmacked and speechless. It was like I wanted to say something but I couldn't. He said take it in and we'll speak tomorrow. I just couldn't take it in. I wanted to say something but just couldn't.'

On what makes José Mourinho The Special One: 'It's honestly everything about the man. First and foremost he is a great man as well, on a personal one-to-one basis he's always there for you. His door is always open both on a personal level and football level. Tactically he's so spot on. We have team meetings. He doesn't waffle on. He says, "Ten-minute meeting. I want you to concentrate." That's it.'

Fantastic

On his head injury in the Carling Cup, and returning from hospital to the Millennium Stadium dressing room: 'I remember walking out for the second half and nothing else until waking up in the ambulance on the way to the hospital. I had the scan and they said it's okay. It was great to be back [with the lads], they were different class. I'm still feeling a bit groggy though. It's thanks to the lads as I didn't have much part to play in the second half. Throughout the competition they've been spot on.'

On the climax to the season – the FA Cup Final at the new Wembley: 'Before kick-off Didier called everyone together and it was a great speech he made. He said that he was nervous, he knew everybody was nervous and we are all feeling the same but one thing was for sure, he was going to fight and give everything for every player in the team. He looked each player in the eye and I think it touched a lot of people.'

… Then climbing the steps to lift the famous trophy: 'It was a long way up there but when you are up there, it is a great view and a great sight seeing all the Chelsea fans waving about. I feel really proud. Walking the last part of that walkway was really special. I was quite emotional. I did feel quite tired when we were celebrating but on an occasion like that, the energy comes from deep inside and that is what we have shown all season. Every captain wanted to be the first walking up those steps. Chelsea were the last at the old Wembley and we were the first at the new and that is special in its own right. Okay, we had won the Carling Cup but I said coming into this game that if we didn't win it, it maybe would have been a disappointing season. It's not, we are on a high now and we go away happy.'

And finally, on his future … maybe as Chelsea's manager!: "I'd certainly like to manage one day. It's certainly the way I want to go, I want to get my [coaching] badges and make that decision at the end of it.'

Crossword

ACROSS

1 Player of the Year 2004 and 2005 (5,7)
4 Claudio Pizarro's other sporting passion (5,6)
11 Chelsea fan who sang the club anthem 'Blue Day' (5)
12 Vegetable banned from the Bridge during the 2007/07 season (6)
13 Scored for his country at the Emirates Stadium in Feb 2007 (8)
16 Steve Sidwell's first professional club (7)
17 Number of times we have won the League title (5)
18 _____ Road, where Stamford Bridge stands (6)
19 The Blues' kit manufacturer (6)
20 _____ Bluewings, our preseason opponents in the USA (5)

DOWN

2 London Olympics supremo and Chelsea supporter (7)
3 Chelsea's new Director of Football (5,5)
5 Home town of José Mourinho (7)
6 Stockport _____, Chelsea's first-ever league opponents in 1905 (6)
7 Grows on the roof of Chelsea's training HQ (5)
8 Florent Malouda's former club (5)
9 Mikel John Obi's country of origin (7)
10 Wayne Bridge's middle name (7)
13 Russian province of which Roman Abramovich is the Governor (8)
14 Highest-ever appearance maker (3,6)
15 _____ Tel Aviv, Tal Ben-Haim's former club (7)

Answers on page 60

Spot The Ball

Use all your expertise and judgement to see if you can 'Spot The Ball'. Answer on page 61.

Chelsea Goal of the

It was a great year for wonder-strikes, so voting for a winner was a tough call. The Chelsea players gave their own verdict on who should top the poll.

Ricardo Carvalho

'Didier Drogba against Liverpool, 1-0. It was a great finish. He turned from the defender and he shoots the ball without seeing the goalkeeper. One turn. A great goal!'

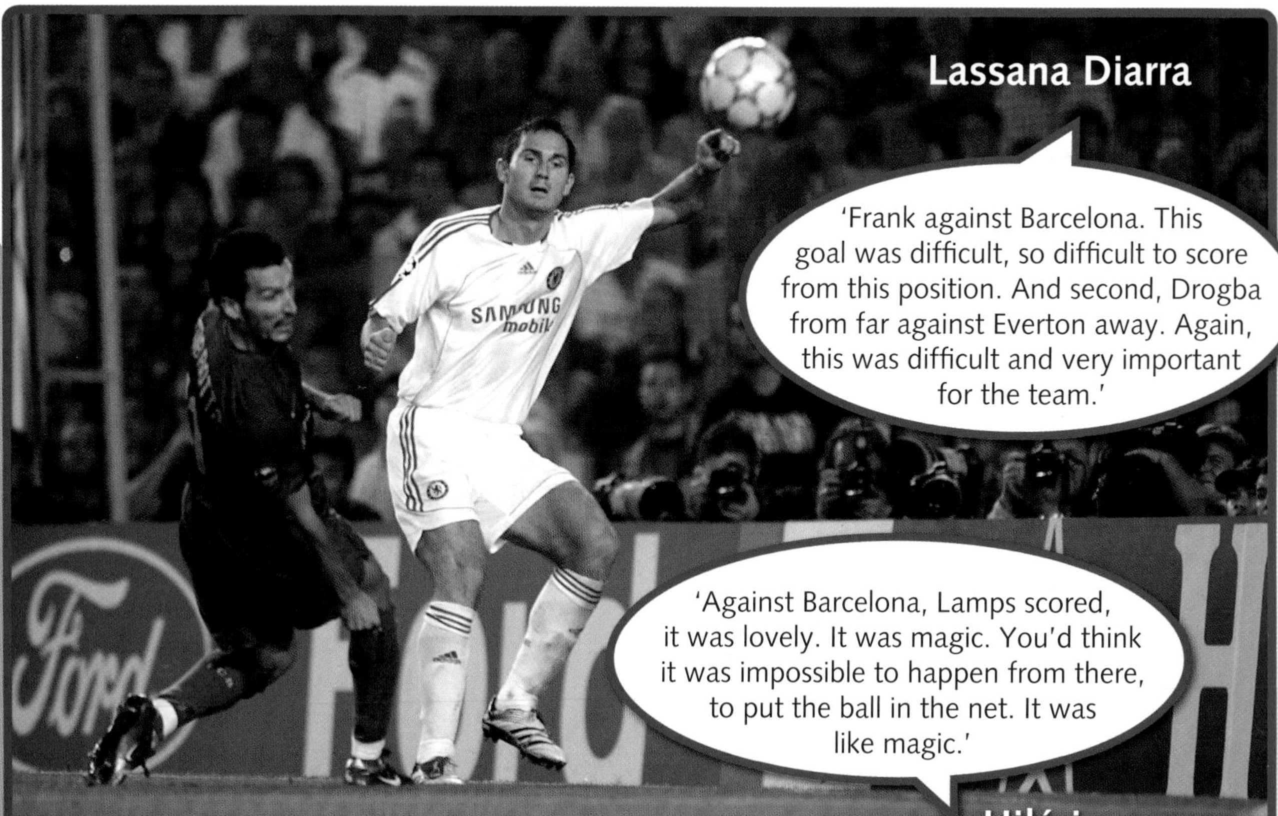

Lassana Diarra

'Frank against Barcelona. This goal was difficult, so difficult to score from this position. And second, Drogba from far against Everton away. Again, this was difficult and very important for the team.'

'Against Barcelona, Lamps scored, it was lovely. It was magic. You'd think it was impossible to happen from there, to put the ball in the net. It was like magic.'

Hilário

Paulo Ferreira

'Drogba at Everton. It was a great goal. For me, it was the best. The shot, the curve that the ball makes, it was unbelievable.'

'Maybe Drogba's against Liverpool. Just the way he turned, he swung and hit it with his left foot. Brilliant!'

John Terry

'Didier's against Liverpool. He battered it on the turn, left foot. Sweet!'

Joe Cole

'Drogba, Liverpool. Backing in, his left and - ya!!'

'Drogba against Everton. It was very, very important to get us the win, and the vision and accuracy needed to shoot from there was unbelievable. And we needed those three points!'

Salomon Kalou

Ashley Cole

'Michael Essien against Arsenal. It was the best shot, it was a goal that was important for the team or we lose.'

Claude Makelele

'Makelele at Tottenham. This is a miracle, first of all because he shoots so strong, and second that he hits the target!!'

Carlo Cudicini

Quiz Answers

Blue Said That?

1. "Of course, the money is fantastic but when I was a youngster coming through I played for nothing and my attitude hasn't changed since then. Take the money away and I would still be the first player into training the following morning."
[Answer: John Terry]

2. "If you're not a big club, you choose one competition and you fight in that competition and forget the others. Big clubs - we cannot do this."
[Answer: José Mourinho]

3. "Playing Chelsea is as tough a test as you'll get in Europe these days."
[Answer: Man United's Michael Carrick]

4. "Lionel Messi is a world-class player. He's young, and chasing him around has done my back in."
[Answer: Ashley Cole]

5. "I feel great. I'm just happy to score the first Cup Final goal in the new stadium. If we didn't win this Cup we would be very, very frustrated."
[Answer: Didier Drogba]

6. "I bought Luna two Chelsea kits, snuck them into the house and put her in one. Elen laughed but took it off and they haven't been out of the drawer since."
[Answer: Frank Lampard]

7. "If you ask every player, they want to play for Chelsea, for that team. It's one of the best teams in the world so I'm very happy to be part of that."
[Answer: Tal Ben-Haim]

Crossword Solution

Wordsearch Solution

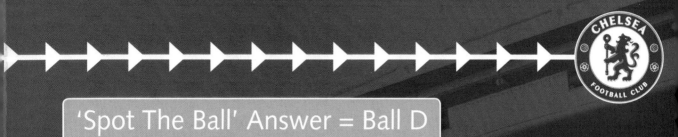

'Spot The Ball' Answer = Ball D

FA Cup Glory →→→→→→

AGAIN!

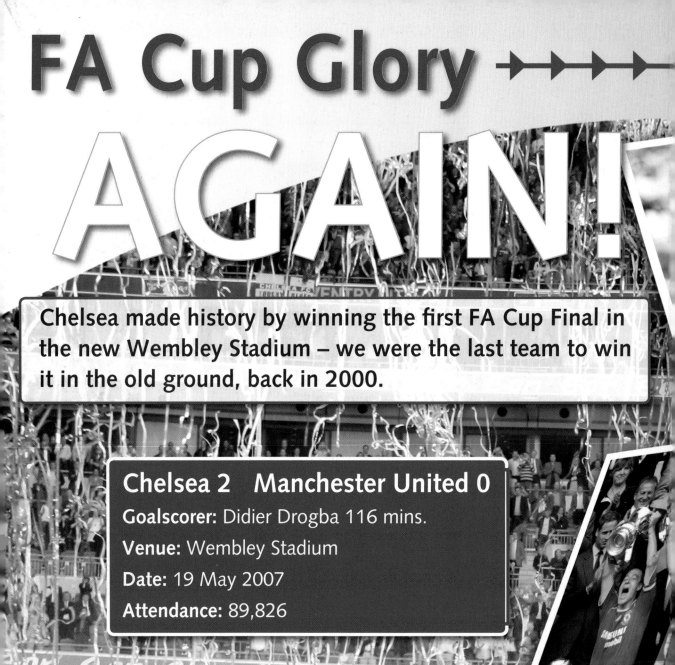

Chelsea made history by winning the first FA Cup Final in the new Wembley Stadium – we were the last team to win it in the old ground, back in 2000.

Chelsea 2   Manchester United 0

Goalscorer: Didier Drogba 116 mins.

Venue: Wembley Stadium

Date: 19 May 2007

Attendance: 89,826